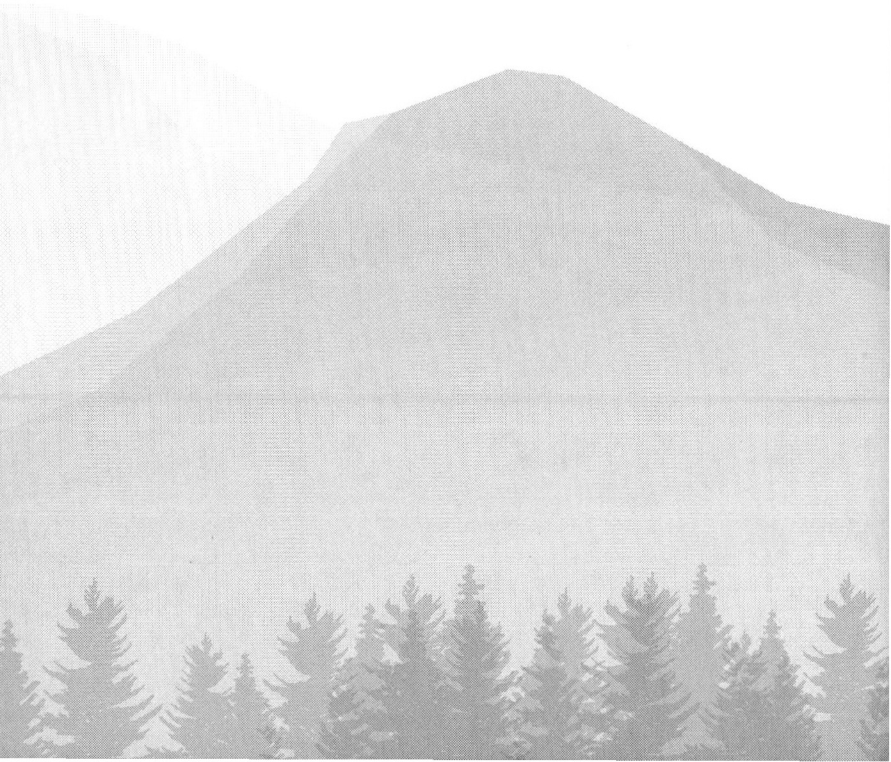

THE INTENTIONAL PURSUIT

DEVOTIONAL

ERICA D BOYD

Copyright © 2024 Turning The Page Publishing, LLC
All rights reserved. No portion of this book may be reproduced, scanned, or distributed in any form without written permission from the publisher, Turning The Page Publishing, LLC.

INTRODUCTION	1
DAY 1: WAKE UP WITH PURPOSE	4
DAY 2: PRIORITIZE WHAT MATTERS	10
DAY 3: THE POWER OF PAUSE	16
DAY 4: ALIGNING YOUR HEART WITH GOD'S WILL	22
DAY 5: EMBRACING THE EVERYDAY MOMENTS	28
DAY 6: EMBRACING GOD'S TIMING	34
DAY 7: THE POWER OF SMALL STEPS	40
DAY 8: CHOOSING THE RIGHT VOICE	46
DAY 9: THE POWER OF SURRENDER	52
DAY 10: THE GIFT OF REST	58
DAY 11: THE BEAUTY OF FORGIVENESS	64
DAY 12: THE STRENGHT OF OBEDIENCE	70
DAY 13: OVERCOMING FEAR WITH FAITH	76
DAY 14: THE WEIGHT OF OUR WORDS	82
DAY 15: TRUSTING GOD IN THE WAITING	88
DAY 16: LIVING WITH CLEAR VISION	94
DAY 17: WALKING IN GOD'S PURPOSE	100
DAY 18: EMBRACING CHANGE	106
DAY 19: THE IMPORTANCE OF PERSISTENCE	112
DAY 20: LIVING WITH PURPOSE AND CLARITY	118
DAY 21: CULTIVATING GRATITUDE	124
DAY 22: WALKING IN INTEGRITY	130
DAY 23: THE POWER OF CONSISTENCY	136
DAY 24: TRUSTING GOD'S PROVISION	142
DAY 25: THE BLESSIN OF GENEROSITY	148
DAY 26: STEPPING INTO GOD'S PLAN FOR YOUR LIFE	154
DAY 27: PURSUING JOY IN ALL THINGS	160
DAY 28: BREAKING FREE FROM COMPARISON	166
DAY 29: THE POWER OF PRAYER IN ACTION	172
DAY 30: LIVING OUT YOUR CALLING	178
DAY 31: THE INTENTIONAL PURSUIT	184
BONUS DAY 32: RELEASING CONTROL TO GOD	192
AFFIRMATIONS OF INTENTIONALITY	199
AFFIRMATION PRAYER	202
CLOSING THOUGHTS	203
CLOSING BLESSING	204

INTRODUCTION

In a world filled with distractions, it's easy to lose sight of what truly matters. We find ourselves caught in the hustle of daily life, reacting to circumstances rather than living with purpose. Yet, deep down, we all long for something more—a life filled with meaning, direction, and clarity. We want to live intentionally, not by accident, but by design.

The Intentional Pursuit: A 31-Day Devotional is a call to reclaim your purpose and live with intention. Each day in this devotional will encourage you to slow down, focus, and seek God's guidance as you navigate the complexities of life. Through powerful scripture, thoughtful reflections, and heartfelt prayers, you will be challenged to align your thoughts, actions, and heart with God's plan for your life.

This devotional is not about perfection, but progress. It's about choosing to live each day with purpose, no matter the season or circumstance. Whether you are in a season of waiting, pursuing dreams, or navigating challenges, you will find wisdom and encouragement here to help you live with clarity and conviction.

As you journey through these 31 days, remember that intentional living begins with small steps. It's about making choices each day that align with your values, your faith, and your God-given purpose. You may not have all the answers, but trust that God is with you every step of the way, guiding you towards the life you were always meant to live.

Are you ready to live with intention? To pursue your purpose with passion? Let's begin this journey together—one day at a time.

DAY 1

WAKE UP WITH PURPOSE

"Teach us to number our days, that we may gain a heart of wisdom."

PSALM 90:12

Every morning is a fresh opportunity—an open door to step into the day with intention. Yet so often, we wake up in a rush, bombarded by the demands of the day before we've even had time to take a breath. We check our phones, scroll through notifications, and dive headfirst into our to-do lists, all while our minds are scattered, and our hearts are disconnected from what truly matters. The pace of life is quick and the distractions are endless. It can feel like there's never enough time to pause, to breathe, or to reflect.

Psalm 90:12 reminds us of the brevity of life. "Teach us to number our days," the psalmist writes. This is not just a prayer for counting the days in the literal sense but a prayer for wisdom in how we live each day. When we are intentional with our time, we recognize that every moment is a chance to align ourselves with God's purpose. If we don't intentionally pause to reflect, we risk living each day as though it's just another 24-hour span to fill, rather than a unique opportunity to live with meaning.

Think about how Jesus lived. He was fully aware of the demands on His time, yet He was intentional in how He spent His days. In Mark 1:35, after a full night of healing and ministering, He wakes early in the morning, before the crowds arrive, and goes to a solitary place to pray. He knew the importance of starting His day centered on the Father. He didn't let the world's expectations dictate His rhythm; He prioritized time with God to gain clarity and strength for the day ahead. This moment wasn't about checking off a box—it was about alignment and purpose. Jesus set the example that intentionality starts in the quiet moments, before the world wakes up and pulls us into its frenzy.

What does it look like to wake up with purpose? It means being present in the moment when we first open our eyes. It means resisting the urge to dive into the noise and instead, choosing to be still and listen. It's about giving God our first thoughts, our first breath, and our first moments. Imagine the difference it would make if, instead of rushing to check off tasks or worry about the day ahead, we took even five minutes to center ourselves in God's presence. These moments of intentional stillness set the foundation for the rest of the day. They equip us with clarity and focus, so we can walk through the day with purpose rather than reactively.

Think of the way you begin your day. Are you truly living with intention, or are you simply existing within the routine? If you feel the weight of your distractions, you're not alone. But God calls us to something deeper—to live each moment with meaning. Each day is an opportunity to ask God, "What would You have me do today? How can I honor You in even the smallest decisions?"

When you wake up tomorrow, take a few moments before your

feet hit the floor. Pause, breathe, and recognize that today is a gift. Ask God for wisdom to live with purpose, to avoid the distractions that pull you away from His will, and to use your time wisely. The way you start your day can shape the way you move through it. The choice is yours—will you choose intentionality or drift through your day?

THE INTENTIONAL PURSUIT: 31 DAY DEVOTIONAL

PRAYER

Heavenly Father, I come before You with a heart that desires to live with purpose, but I know how easily I can become distracted by the demands and noise of life. I confess that too often I rush through my mornings without acknowledging You. I allow the world to dictate my pace, and I miss the opportunity to begin my day with intention.

Lord, teach me to slow down. Help me to recognize that my days are precious, that every moment is an opportunity to walk in Your purpose. Give me wisdom to make each day count, to live with a heart that's focused on You, not the distractions. Help me start my mornings in stillness, before the busyness of the world takes over. I want to give You the first moments of my day, trusting that when I align my heart with You, the rest of my day will follow with clarity and purpose.

Please guide my thoughts, my decisions, and my actions today. Help me to be present, to live intentionally, and to use my time in a way that honors You. I don't want to merely go through the motions of life—I want to live with meaning, to make every moment matter. Thank You for the gift of today, and for the grace to start again. Amen.

INTENTIONAL REFLECTION

What is one way you can start your day tomorrow with intention? How can you make the first few moments of your day count for something greater?

Feel free to take a moment and write down your thoughts and ideas.

THE INTENTIONAL PURSUIT: 31 DAY DEVOTIONAL

DAY 2

PRIORITIZE WHAT MATTERS

"But seek first the kingdom of God and His righteousness, and all these things will be added to you."

MATTHEW 6:33

Life has a way of pulling us in many directions. From our jobs and responsibilities to our relationships and personal goals, it can feel like we're juggling endless tasks, each demanding our time and attention. As a result, we often find ourselves overwhelmed, stretching ourselves thin, trying to please everyone and keep up with every expectation. In the process, we lose sight of what truly matters.

Matthew 6:33 offers us a powerful reminder: when we focus on seeking God first, everything else falls into place. Jesus doesn't promise that everything will be easy or that all our desires will be fulfilled in the way we expect. But He assures us that when we prioritize God and His will above all else, He will provide for us and give us the wisdom to navigate life's demands.

We often seek success, comfort, and approval in our own strength, believing that achieving those things will bring us peace and fulfillment. But Jesus flips that narrative. He calls us to seek His kingdom first. To be intentional about where we direct our time, energy, and hearts. When we make God our priority, our perspective changes. Suddenly, everything we do—whether it's our work, our relationships, or our personal goals—takes on a new meaning because it's aligned with His purpose for us.

Think about the story of Martha and Mary in Luke 10:38-42. Martha was busy with all the details of hosting, while her sister Mary chose to sit at Jesus' feet and listen to Him. Martha was anxious, worried about getting everything just right, but Jesus gently reminded her that Mary had chosen the better part. In that moment, Mary wasn't focused on the tasks that seemed urgent; she was focused on what mattered most—being in the presence of Jesus. Jesus wasn't dismissing the importance of the work Martha was doing, but He was reminding her that the work would have been more meaningful if it was rooted in time spent with Him.

We, too, often get caught up in the rush of responsibilities and to-do lists. We may feel the weight of needing to accomplish everything, but we can't forget the most important thing: being present with God. Our busyness doesn't define us—our relationship with Him does. We must intentionally choose to put God first in the midst of our daily routines, allowing Him to lead us, guide us, and give us the clarity to know what truly matters.

The key to intentional living is this: It's not about doing more or checking off more tasks. It's about making intentional choices, day by day, to seek God above all else. It's about setting priorities that honor Him. When we make time for God—whether through prayer, reading Scripture, or simply being still in His presence—we align our hearts with His, and the rest of our day naturally follows in that rhythm.

As you go through today, take a moment to reflect on where

your time and energy are going. Are you giving your attention to the things that matter most, or are you allowing the busyness of life to dictate your pace? Are you intentionally making room for God, or are you letting other things take His place?

PRAYER

Father, I confess that I often let the demands of life take over, and I lose sight of what truly matters. It's so easy to get caught up in the rush, to focus on what's urgent rather than what's important. Help me to prioritize You above all else. Teach me to seek Your kingdom first, to make time for You in the midst of the busyness, and to trust that when I do, everything else will fall into place.

God, I know that You're not asking me to abandon my responsibilities, but to approach them with the right heart and the right focus. Give me the wisdom to discern what truly matters today. Help me to spend my time wisely and to invest in the things that align with Your will for my life. Show me where I need to let go of distractions and make room for You.

Lord, I want my life to reflect Your love and purpose. Help me to live intentionally, choosing You first in every decision I make. Thank You for Your faithfulness and for the reminder that You will provide for me when I seek You above all else. Amen.

INTENTIONAL REFLECTION

How can you intentionally prioritize God in the midst of your busy day? What is one action you can take today to focus more on His kingdom than your own to-do list?

Feel free to take a moment and write down your thoughts and ideas.

THE INTENTIONAL PURSUIT: 31 DAY DEVOTIONAL

DAY 3

THE POWER OF PAUSE

"Be still, and know that I am God."

PSALM 46:10

We live in a world that celebrates busyness. The more tasks we juggle, the more responsibilities we take on, the more "important" we feel. It seems that the value we place on productivity has overtaken the value we place on rest. We live our days in constant motion, driven by deadlines, expectations, and self-imposed pressures. But what if the key to intentional living isn't doing more, but doing less? What if we could change the narrative by allowing space for stillness?

Psalm 46:10 invites us to "be still" and reminds us that in that stillness, we can recognize that God is sovereign. This stillness isn't about idle time or avoidance; it's a conscious choice to create space for God to speak into our lives. In a world full of noise and distractions, it's easy to forget that sometimes the most powerful thing we can do is stop, breathe, and allow ourselves to rest in God's presence.

In 1 Kings 19:11-13, Elijah finds himself at a breaking point. He's been running, fleeing from danger, overwhelmed by exhaustion and fear. God tells him to go to the mountain and wait. When Elijah arrives, a mighty wind comes, followed by an earthquake and fire.

But God isn't in any of those dramatic events. Instead, God speaks in a gentle whisper. This moment teaches us that while we're often chasing big signs, God is often present in the quiet and the still.

God desires to meet us in the quiet places of our hearts. He wants us to experience His presence, not in the rush of the day but in the stillness of our souls. When we stop to pause—whether in prayer, contemplation, or simply sitting in silence—we create space for God to direct our steps, renew our strength, and give us clarity.

Intentional living begins with the power of pause. In those moments of stillness, we find God's direction for the day. We recalibrate our minds and hearts to His will. So, instead of rushing through your day today, take a moment to stop. Breathe. Be still. Know that He is God, and in His presence, you will find peace.

THE INTENTIONAL PURSUIT: 31 DAY DEVOTIONAL

PRAYER

Father, I confess that I often get caught up in the hustle and bustle of life, constantly moving from one thing to the next without ever truly stopping. I forget the power of stillness, the beauty of being present with You. Help me to slow down today and make space for Your voice. Teach me how to pause and listen to Your gentle whisper amidst the noise of my daily life.

God, I want to experience Your peace in a world that's constantly in motion. Give me the courage to step back, to stop striving, and to rest in Your presence. May my time of stillness be a reminder that You are in control, and that You are always with me, even when I'm not doing anything. Guide me today, and help me to walk in Your peace. Amen.

INTENTIONAL REFLECTION

What is one moment today that you can intentionally pause and be still before God? How can you create space for stillness in your routine?

Feel free to take a moment and write down your thoughts and ideas.

THE INTENTIONAL PURSUIT: 31 DAY DEVOTIONAL

DAY 4

ALIGNING YOUR HEART WITH GOD'S WILL

"Commit your work to the Lord, and your plans will be established."

PROVERBS 16:3

We all have plans. Whether it's a career goal, a personal dream, or the small tasks we set out to accomplish each day, our lives are full of intentions. But how often do we stop to ask whether our plans are aligned with God's will? It's easy to go through life simply doing what we think is best, driven by our desires, ambitions, and what the world says we should do. But God's Word calls us to something deeper: to align our hearts with His will and trust that He will guide our steps.

Proverbs 16:3 tells us that when we commit our work to the Lord, our plans will be established. This isn't just about praying for God's blessing on our own plans; it's about surrendering our desires and goals to Him and trusting that He knows the best path for us. It's acknowledging that God's purpose for us may not always align with our own expectations, but His way is always better.

In the life of Jesus, we see the ultimate example of surrender. In Matthew 26:39, as He faces the impending agony of the cross, Jesus prays, "Not as I will, but as You will." Despite His personal anguish and the difficulty ahead, He surrenders His own desires to the will of His Father. Jesus' commitment to God's will wasn't just a one-time decision—it was a daily, ongoing act of surrender.

Aligning our hearts with God's will doesn't always come easily. It requires us to lay down our own agendas, to trust in God's timing, and to believe that His plans are far greater than anything we could imagine. But when we choose to commit our work, our dreams, and our everyday decisions to Him, we can rest in the assurance that He will guide us toward His purpose.

Living intentionally means inviting God into every part of our day—every decision, every task, every moment. It's about trusting that when we align our hearts with His, He will establish our steps and lead us to places we could never go on our own.

THE INTENTIONAL PURSUIT: 31 DAY DEVOTIONAL

PRAYER

Father, I acknowledge that I often make plans without fully considering Your will. I confess that I can be quick to pursue my own desires without asking for Your guidance. Lord, I want to commit my work to You. I want to align my heart with Your will and trust that You will establish my steps.

Help me to surrender my plans to You, even when it's difficult. Give me the courage to let go of my own agenda and to trust that Your way is better. Show me the path You have for me and help me to walk in it with faith. I want to live a life that reflects Your purpose, not my own. Thank You for Your guidance and for the assurance that You will lead me when I seek Your will. Amen.

ERICA D. BOYD

INTENTIONAL REFLECTION

What areas of your life do you need to align with God's will today? How can you intentionally surrender your plans and trust Him more fully?

Feel free to take a moment and write down your thoughts and ideas.

THE INTENTIONAL PURSUIT: 31 DAY DEVOTIONAL

DAY 5

EMBRACING THE EVERYDAY MOMENTS

"So whether you eat or drink, or whatever you do, do all to the glory of God."

1 CORINTHIANS 10:30

It's easy to think that living intentionally requires big, dramatic moments—those life-changing decisions or grand acts of service. But the truth is, most of our days are filled with ordinary, mundane tasks. We wake up, go to work, make meals, clean our homes, and handle the small but necessary things of life. It's easy to overlook the significance of these tasks, but Scripture reminds us that everything we do—big or small—can be done to the glory of God.

In 1 Corinthians 10:31, Paul encourages us to do everything, even the most ordinary tasks, for God's glory. This means that the work we do, the conversations we have, and the ways we interact with others should reflect God's love and purpose. Living intentionally isn't just about making big decisions; it's about making everyday moments count.

When we look at the life of Jesus, we see that He didn't just do extraordinary things in extraordinary places. He interacted with people in everyday settings. He ate meals with sinners (Luke 19:1-10), He healed the sick, He taught in synagogues, but He also did simple things like walking with His disciples and sharing a meal. Jesus didn't just make His life about the big moments; He made every moment count by doing everything with love, humility, and purpose.

In the same way, we can find meaning in our everyday actions. Whether we're cooking dinner, running errands, or responding to an email, we can do those things with intention, seeking to honor God in all of it.

Living intentionally means finding purpose in the present, no matter how simple it seems. It's about shifting your mindset to see God's hand in the small things and choosing to honor Him in every task, conversation, or decision. Intentional living requires recognizing that every moment, no matter how ordinary, carries the potential to glorify God and impact others.

THE INTENTIONAL PURSUIT: 31 DAY DEVOTIONAL

PRAYER

Lord, I confess that I often overlook the everyday moments, thinking that they don't matter in the grand scheme of things. But today, I choose to embrace the ordinary as an opportunity to honor You. Help me to see the beauty in the mundane and to approach every task, big or small, with intention.

I want to do all things to Your glory, even when it seems insignificant. Teach me to bring Your presence into the everyday moments, to live with purpose in every conversation, every chore, and every decision. Thank You for reminding me that even the smallest actions can reflect Your love. Help me to make every moment count for You. Amen.

INTENTIONAL REFLECTION

How can you bring intentionality to the everyday moments in your life today? What small task can you turn into an opportunity to glorify God?

Feel free to take a moment and write down your thoughts and ideas.

THE INTENTIONAL PURSUIT: 31 DAY DEVOTIONAL

DAY 6

EMBRACING GOD'S TIMING

"There is a time for everything, and a season for every activity under the heavens."

ECCLESIASTES 3:1

In our fast-paced world, it's easy to become impatient. We want things to happen quickly—our career goals, our personal dreams, and even our everyday tasks. Waiting can feel like a waste of time, and we often feel frustrated when things don't happen on our schedule. But what if God has a purpose in the waiting? What if His timing is perfect, and what we see as delays are actually opportunities for growth?

Ecclesiastes 3:1 tells us that there is a time and season for everything. The reality is, we don't control the clock. We don't set the calendar. And while we can plan and work toward our goals, there are moments when we need to trust that God's timing is better than our own. Sometimes, the right opportunities come at the right time—often when we least expect them, but always at the perfect moment.

Consider the story of Abraham and Sarah (Genesis 17). God promised them a child, but they didn't receive that promise for many years. In the meantime, they grew impatient and tried to take matters into their own hands, which led to complications and challenges. But when the time came, God fulfilled His promise, and they had a son, Isaac. The lesson here is that even though Abraham and Sarah's waiting was long, God's timing was perfect. Had they rushed the process, they might have missed the blessing.

Living intentionally means trusting God's perfect timing. It means learning to embrace the seasons of waiting and trusting that God is doing something in those moments—building our patience, character, and faith. Instead of pushing for our own timeline, we must learn to lean into His. God is never late, and He is never early. He is always right on time.

PRAYER

Father, I confess that I often struggle with impatience. I want things to happen on my time, but I know Your timing is always perfect. Help me to trust You more deeply in the waiting. Teach me to embrace the seasons of life, knowing that You are working behind the scenes, even when I can't see it.

Lord, I surrender my timelines to You. I give You my plans, my dreams, and my desires. Help me to have patience and faith in Your timing. May I rest in the assurance that You are always on time, and that Your plans for me are good. I trust that You are orchestrating every detail of my life, and that You are working all things for my good. Thank You for Your perfect timing. Amen.

INTENTIONAL REFLECTION

What areas of your life are you trying to rush? How can you embrace God's timing instead of your own?

Feel free to take a moment and write down your thoughts and ideas.

THE INTENTIONAL PURSUIT: 31 DAY DEVOTIONAL

DAY 7

THE POWER OF SMALL STEPS

"If you are faithful in little things, you will be faithful in large ones."

LUKE 16:10 (NLT)

Often, we want the big, dramatic change—the breakthrough moment that shifts everything at once. We dream of instant transformation, the big promotion, or the large project completed in a flash. But the reality is that most progress happens through small, consistent steps that add up over time. Every journey is made up of smaller, manageable pieces that, when added together, form a bigger picture.

In Luke 16:10, Jesus teaches us that faithfulness in the small things prepares us for the larger things. It's easy to overlook the significance of small tasks or dismiss them as unimportant. Yet, these are the very moments that God uses to build our character, develop our discipline, and strengthen our perseverance. The small steps we take in faith are not insignificant in His eyes. In fact, they are the building blocks of greater responsibility and greater impact.

Consider the story of David, who was anointed to be king over Israel, but before he wore a crown, he was a shepherd. He didn't skip over the mundane task of tending sheep to jump straight into kingship. His time as a shepherd was essential in preparing him for the responsibilities of leading a nation. David's faithfulness in the small, unnoticed tasks prepared him for the great battle with Goliath, and eventually, for ruling Israel. It was through his small steps of obedience and faithfulness to God's call that David grew into the leader he was destined to become.

Living intentionally means embracing the process, even when it feels like your efforts are small or slow. It means being faithful with what God has given you right now, knowing that your consistency in the small things builds the foundation for something greater. The journey to your dreams and goals might not always be glamorous, but each small step is moving you forward, building momentum, and developing the character you need for what's to come.

ERICA D. BOYD

THE INTENTIONAL PURSUIT: 31 DAY DEVOTIONAL

PRAYER

Lord, I confess that I often want immediate results and instant gratification. Help me to embrace the small steps, knowing that they matter in Your eyes. Teach me to be faithful in the little things and to trust that each small act is preparing me for the greater things You have planned for my life.

When I feel discouraged by the pace of progress, remind me that You are with me in every step. Strengthen my patience and perseverance, and help me to stay focused on living intentionally, no matter how small the task may seem. Just as David was faithful in the fields before he led Israel, help me to be faithful in the tasks You've placed before me. Thank You for using these moments to shape me and prepare me for what lies ahead. In Jesus' name, Amen.

ERICA D. BOYD

INTENTIONAL REFLECTION

What small step can you take today toward your long-term goals? How can you embrace the importance of being faithful in the little things?

Feel free to take a moment and write down your thoughts and ideas.

THE INTENTIONAL PURSUIT: 31 DAY DEVOTIONAL

DAY 8

CHOOSING THE RIGHT VOICE

"My sheep listen to my voice; I know them, they follow me."

JOHN 10:27

Every day, we are surrounded by countless voices competing for our attention—the opinions of others, societal pressures, social media, and even our own doubts and insecurities. These voices can become so loud that they drown out the one voice we truly need to hear: God's. If we are not intentional, the noise around us will lead us away from His purpose and into confusion, anxiety, and misplaced priorities.

In 1 Kings 19:11-13, we find the prophet Elijah in a moment of fear and despair, running from his enemies. He desperately needed to hear from God. But when God revealed Himself to Elijah, it wasn't in the powerful wind, the earthquake, or the fire—it was in a gentle whisper. Elijah had to quiet his heart and focus to hear God's voice. This story reminds us that God often speaks not through the loud and dramatic but through the still, small moments. To hear Him, we must intentionally tune out the noise and seek His presence.

Think about the voices influencing your decisions and shaping your thoughts. Are they pointing you toward God's truth, or are they pulling you in another direction? The world may tell you to chase success, seek validation, or conform to its standards. But God's voice calls you to peace, purpose, and an identity rooted in Him. The more time you spend in His Word and in prayer, the easier it becomes to recognize His voice amidst the noise.

Living intentionally means choosing the right voice—the voice of God. It's about prioritizing time in His presence, where you can hear His guidance, experience His peace, and be reminded of His love. This week, take inventory of the voices you've been listening to. Are they drawing you closer to God, or do they leave you feeling overwhelmed and empty? Make it your goal to quiet the noise and tune into God's gentle whisper.

ERICA D. BOYD

PRAYER

Lord, in the midst of the noise and chaos of life, I long to hear Your voice. Teach me to recognize Your gentle whisper and to turn down the volume of everything else that competes for my attention. I confess that I often let distractions and other voices drown out Your truth. Forgive me for the times I've prioritized the world over Your Word.

Father, help me to seek You intentionally each day. Give me discernment to identify the voices that align with Your will and courage to let go of the ones that don't. I want to follow You, to know Your voice, and to trust Your guidance in every area of my life. Thank You for always speaking, even when I fail to listen. I choose today to tune into Your voice above all else. Amen.

ERICA D. BOYD

INTENTIONAL REFLECTION

What voices have been influencing your thoughts and decisions recently? How can you make space to hear God's voice more clearly?

Feel free to take a moment and write down your thoughts and ideas.

THE INTENTIONAL PURSUIT: 31 DAY DEVOTIONAL

DAY 9

THE POWER OF SURRENDER

"Trust in the Lord with all your heart and lean not on your own understanding; in all your ways submit to him, and he will make your paths straight."

PROVERBS 3:5-6

Control gives us a sense of security. Whether it's planning our future, managing relationships, or navigating challenges, being in control makes us feel powerful and prepared. But what happens when life throws us curve balls we didn't anticipate? When our plans fall apart, or the path forward becomes unclear? These moments remind us of one undeniable truth: we are not in control, but God is.

Surrendering to God can feel like stepping into the unknown. It requires us to trust Him with the details of our lives—the things we hold closest to our hearts. Consider Abraham's story in Genesis 22, when God asked him to sacrifice his beloved son, Isaac. This request must have been agonizing, yet Abraham chose to obey, believing in God's faithfulness. At the last moment, God provided a ram in Isaac's place, showing Abraham that surrender doesn't lead to loss but to God's provision and purpose.

Surrender isn't a one-time act; it's a daily decision. It means giving God control over the areas of your life that you're tempted to micromanage—your career, relationships, finances, or even your fears and disappointments. It doesn't mean abandoning responsibility but acknowledging that God's plans are higher than your own. When you surrender, you invite God to take the lead, trusting that He knows what's best even when you don't understand.

Living intentionally starts with surrender. It's about laying down your desires, your expectations, and your fears at God's feet, trusting that He is working for your good. What are you holding onto too tightly today? Choose to let go and let God.

THE INTENTIONAL PURSUIT: 31 DAY DEVOTIONAL

PRAYER

Heavenly Father, I come to You with open hands and an open heart. I confess that I often try to take control, holding tightly to my plans and my understanding. But today, I choose to surrender. I trust that Your ways are higher than mine and that You are working all things together for my good.

Help me to lay down my fears, my doubts, and my need for control. Teach me to rest in the assurance that You are faithful and that Your plans for me are good. Even when I don't understand, I choose to trust You. Thank You for being my guide, my provider, and my refuge. I surrender every part of my life into Your hands. Amen.

INTENTIONAL REFLECTION

What area of your life is hardest to surrender to God? What steps can you take today to release control and trust Him fully?

Feel free to take a moment and write down your thoughts and ideas.

THE INTENTIONAL PURSUIT: 31 DAY DEVOTIONAL

DAY 10

THE GIFT OF REST

"Come to me, all you who are weary and burdened, and I will give you rest."

MATTHEW 11:28

In a world that values productivity and hustle, rest often feels like a luxury we can't afford. We pack our schedules to the brim, constantly striving to accomplish more, to prove our worth, and to meet expectations. But this relentless pursuit of "doing" can leave us feeling exhausted, unfulfilled, and disconnected from God's peace.

Jesus' invitation in Matthew 11:28 is a reminder that rest is not just a physical need—it's a spiritual one. Resting in God means stepping away from the chaos of life and finding renewal in His presence. In Exodus 20:8-11, God instituted the Sabbath, a day of rest, as a commandment. Why? Because He knows our tendency to overwork, overcommit, and overlook the importance of pausing to recharge.

Imagine the disciples in Mark 6:30-32. After a busy season of ministry, Jesus called them away to a quiet place to rest. Even though there was still work to be done, Jesus recognized their need to refuel. This story reminds us that rest isn't selfish or lazy—it's necessary for us to function well and fulfill God's purpose for our lives.

Living intentionally means honoring the gift of rest. It's about recognizing when you're running on empty and giving yourself permission to slow down. It's not just about napping or taking a vacation; it's about creating space for God to restore your soul. When was the last time you truly rested in His presence?

THE INTENTIONAL PURSUIT: 31 DAY DEVOTIONAL

PRAYER

Lord, thank You for inviting me to find rest in You. I confess that I often neglect this gift, filling my time with busyness and leaving little room for stillness. Teach me to embrace rest as an act of faith and trust in Your provision.

Help me to lay down the burdens I'm carrying and to stop striving in my own strength. Renew my spirit, restore my energy, and remind me that my worth is not found in what I do but in who I am in You. Thank You for being my source of peace and restoration. Today, I choose to rest in Your presence. Amen.

INTENTIONAL REFLECTION

What is one way you can prioritize rest this week? How can resting in God's presence renew your strength?

Feel free to take a moment and write down your thoughts and ideas.

THE INTENTIONAL PURSUIT: 31 DAY DEVOTIONAL

DAY 11

THE BEAUTY OF FORGIVENESS

"Be kind and compassionate to one another, forgiving each other, just as in Christ God forgave you"

EPHESIANS 4:32

Forgiveness is a concept we all admire but often struggle to practice. When someone wrongs us, the pain can cut deep, leaving scars that seem impossible to heal. The idea of forgiving them can feel like letting them off the hook or minimizing the hurt they caused. But forgiveness is not about excusing someone's behavior—it's about freeing yourself from the weight of bitterness and allowing God's love to flow through you.

Consider the story of the prodigal son (Luke 15:11-32). After squandering his inheritance and living recklessly, the son returned home, expecting condemnation. Instead, his father welcomed him with open arms, demonstrating a level of grace and forgiveness that mirrors God's love for us. This story challenges us to forgive as we have been forgiven, even when it feels undeserved.

Forgiveness is a choice, not a feeling. It doesn't mean forgetting the pain or reconciling in every situation. Instead, it's about releasing the offense to God and trusting Him to bring justice and healing. Unforgiveness keeps us trapped in a cycle of anger and resentment, but forgiveness sets us free.

Living intentionally means choosing forgiveness, even when it's hard. It's about letting go of the past so you can step into the future God has for you. Who do you need to forgive today? Ask God to soften your heart and guide you toward freedom.

PRAYER

Father, forgiveness is not always easy. I confess that I sometimes hold onto bitterness and let the pain of the past weigh me down. But I know that You call me to forgive, just as You have forgiven me.

Help me to release the hurt and to trust You with the healing process. Give me the courage to extend grace, even when it feels undeserved. Thank You for Your endless mercy and for the example of forgiveness You've shown through Christ. I choose today to walk in freedom, letting go of bitterness and embracing Your peace. Amen.

ERICA D. BOYD

INTENTIONAL REFLECTION

Who is God asking you to forgive, and how can you begin that process today?

Feel free to take a moment and write down your thoughts and ideas.

THE INTENTIONAL PURSUIT: 31 DAY DEVOTIONAL

DAY 12

THE STRENGHT OF OBEDIENCE

"But Samuel replied, 'Does the Lord delight in burnt offerings and sacrifices as much as in obeying the Lord? To obey is better than sacrifice, and to heed is better than the fat of rams.'"

1 SAMUEL 15:22

Obedience can be challenging, especially when it requires us to trust God's instructions over our own desires or understanding. We might rationalize our actions, thinking we're doing enough for God through our sacrifices, talents, or good deeds. But God desires more than outward offerings—He desires a heart surrendered to Him in full obedience.

In 1 Samuel 15, King Saul was commanded to completely destroy the Amalekites and their possessions. Yet, Saul decided to keep some of the spoils, rationalizing that they could be offered as sacrifices to God. His disobedience cost him the kingdom because he valued his own judgment over God's command. This story teaches us that partial obedience is still disobedience, and it reminds us that God sees our hearts more than our actions.

Living intentionally means aligning your life with God's will, even when it's uncomfortable or inconvenient. Sometimes obedience means waiting when you want to move forward or letting go when you want to hold on. Other times, it means stepping out in faith, even when the path is unclear. Obedience isn't always easy, but it's always worth it because it leads to deeper intimacy with God and positions you for His blessings.

THE INTENTIONAL PURSUIT: 31 DAY DEVOTIONAL

PRAYER

Lord, I confess that obedience is not always easy for me. I often lean on my own understanding, trying to make decisions that seem right in my eyes. But I know Your ways are higher than mine, and Your plans are always good.

Help me to trust You completely, even when I don't understand the "why" behind Your instructions. Give me the strength to obey You fully, not just in the big things but in the small, daily choices. Teach me to value Your approval over the opinions of others and to seek Your will above my own desires. Thank You for loving me enough to guide me in the right direction. Today, I choose to surrender my heart to You in obedience. Amen.

INTENTIONAL REFLECTION

Is there an area in your life where you've been hesitant to obey God? What steps can you take today to align your heart and actions with His will?

Feel free to take a moment and write down your thoughts and ideas.

THE INTENTIONAL PURSUIT: 31 DAY DEVOTIONAL

DAY 13

OVERCOMING FEAR WITH FAITH

"For God has not given us a spirit of fear, but of power, love, and a sound mind."

2 TIMOTHY 1:7

Fear is a universal experience. It comes in many forms—fear of failure, rejection, the unknown, or even fear of stepping out into God's calling for your life. While fear can protect us from real danger, it often becomes a barrier that keeps us from living fully and faithfully.

Consider the story of Gideon in Judges 6. When God called Gideon to lead Israel against the Midianites, he was filled with doubt and fear. He saw himself as the weakest in his family, unqualified for such a task. Yet, God assured him, "I will be with you, and you will strike down all the Midianites, leaving none alive" (Judges 6:16). Despite his fear, Gideon took small, courageous steps of faith, eventually leading Israel to victory.

Like Gideon, you might feel unqualified or overwhelmed by the challenges ahead. But fear doesn't come from God—it's a tool the enemy uses to keep you stagnant. God has equipped you with power, love, and a sound mind to face whatever comes your way. Faith doesn't mean the absence of fear; it means choosing to trust God in the midst of it.

Living intentionally means refusing to let fear dictate your decisions. It's about trusting that God's power is greater than your insecurities and stepping out in faith, even when it feels uncomfortable. What fear is holding you back today? Surrender it to God, and take one step forward, trusting that He is with you.

PRAYER

Heavenly Father, fear often tries to take hold of my heart and my decisions. I confess that I sometimes allow it to paralyze me, keeping me from stepping into the plans You have for me. But today, I choose faith over fear.

Thank You for reminding me that You have not given me a spirit of fear, but of power, love, and a sound mind. Help me to lean on Your strength when I feel weak and to trust Your promises when I feel uncertain. Guide my steps and give me courage to face the challenges ahead, knowing that You are with me every step of the way. I surrender my fears to You, Lord, and I choose to walk forward in faith. Amen.

INTENTIONAL REFLECTION

What fear has been holding you back from fully trusting God? How can you take a step of faith today to move past it?

Feel free to take a moment and write down your thoughts and ideas.

_____
_____
_____
_____
_____
_____
_____
_____
_____
_____
_____
_____
_____
_____
_____
_____
_____
_____
_____
_____

THE INTENTIONAL PURSUIT: 31 DAY DEVOTIONAL

DAY 14

THE WEIGHT OF OUR WORDS

"The tongue has the power of life and death, and those who love it will eat its fruit."

PROVERBS 18:21

Have you ever spoken something in frustration or anger, only to regret it later? Our words carry immense power. They can uplift or tear down, inspire or discourage, heal or wound. Proverbs reminds us that our tongues hold the power of life and death, urging us to choose our words carefully and intentionally.

Consider the story of Peter in Matthew 26:69-75. When faced with the fear of persecution, Peter denied knowing Jesus—not once, but three times. His words betrayed his faith in that moment, but later, his regret drove him to repentance. By the time we see Peter in Acts 2, his words are transformed into a bold declaration of faith, leading thousands to salvation. This shift reminds us that while our words may fail us at times, God can redeem them for His purpose.

Living intentionally means being mindful of the impact of your words. It's choosing to build others up rather than tear them down and speaking life instead of spreading negativity. It also means examining the words you speak to yourself. Negative self-talk can paralyze you, but declaring God's truth over your life brings freedom and confidence. Intentional living calls for words that reflect God's love, truth, and grace in every interaction.

THE INTENTIONAL PURSUIT: 31 DAY DEVOTIONAL

PRAYER

Lord, thank You for the gift of words and the ability to communicate with others. I confess that I have not always used my words wisely. I've spoken in anger, frustration, or carelessness, and I know these words can leave lasting wounds. Please forgive me and help me to choose my words with care.

Teach me to speak life—to encourage, uplift, and inspire others with my words. Help me to speak Your truth over myself, rejecting negativity and embracing the identity You've given me. Let my words reflect Your love and bring healing wherever they're needed. Thank You for the power You've entrusted to me through my words. May I use them to glorify You. Amen.

INTENTIONAL REFLECTION

How can you use your words more intentionally to speak life into yourself and others today?

Feel free to take a moment and write down your thoughts and ideas.

THE INTENTIONAL PURSUIT: 31 DAY DEVOTIONAL

DAY 15

TRUSTING GOD IN THE WAITING

"Wait for the Lord; be strong and take heart and wait for the Lord."

PSALM 27:14

Waiting is one of the hardest things to do. Whether it's waiting for a breakthrough, an answer to prayer, or a season of change, the in-between can feel frustrating and lonely. We live in a world that values instant gratification, but God often works on a different timetable, using the waiting to refine us, deepen our trust, and prepare us for what's ahead.

The story of Joseph is a powerful example of God's purpose in the waiting. Sold into slavery by his brothers, wrongfully imprisoned, and forgotten by those he helped, Joseph could have easily given up on God's promises. Yet, through every trial, Joseph remained faithful. When the time was right, God elevated him to second-in-command in Egypt, using him to save countless lives during a famine (Genesis 41). Looking back, Joseph could see how God's hand was at work, even in the moments when it felt like nothing was happening.

Living intentionally means embracing the waiting seasons as part of God's divine plan. It's trusting that He is working behind the scenes, even when you don't see immediate results. Intentional living involves using the waiting period to grow in faith, seek His presence, and prepare for what's ahead. Instead of rushing ahead or losing hope, you choose to remain steadfast, knowing His timing is perfect.

If you're in a season of waiting, take heart. God is not ignoring you. He sees you, He hears you, and He is working behind the scenes for your good. Let this time draw you closer to Him, and trust that His plan is worth the wait.

THE INTENTIONAL PURSUIT: 31 DAY DEVOTIONAL

PRAYER

Father, waiting is hard. It challenges my patience, my faith, and my trust in Your timing. I confess that I often want things to happen on my schedule, but I know that Your timing is perfect. Thank You for reminding me that waiting is not wasted when I trust You.

Help me to find peace in the in-between, knowing that You are working even when I can't see it. Strengthen my faith and teach me to rest in Your promises. Give me the courage to wait well, with a heart that remains hopeful and expectant. Thank You for being a faithful God who never forgets His children. I choose to trust You, even in the waiting. Amen.

INTENTIONAL REFLECTION

What are you waiting on God for right now? How can you use this season of waiting to grow closer to Him?

Feel free to take a moment and write down your thoughts and ideas.

THE INTENTIONAL PURSUIT: 31 DAY DEVOTIONAL

DAY 16

LIVING WITH CLEAR VISION

"Where there is no vision, the people perish."

PROVERBS 29:18 (KJV)

Having a clear vision is essential to living intentionally. Without a clear direction, we can easily get caught up in the busyness of life without making any progress toward what truly matters. Vision is not just about seeing where you want to go; it's about understanding why you're going there and being clear on the purpose behind it.

In the Bible, Nehemiah is a prime example of living with a clear vision. When he heard about the broken walls of Jerusalem, he was deeply moved and felt a responsibility to rebuild them. Despite facing tremendous opposition, Nehemiah remained focused on his mission, trusting in God's plan for his life. He didn't let distractions or discouragement pull him off track. He knew that God had called him to restore the walls, and nothing was going to stop him from fulfilling that vision.

Living intentionally means having a vision for your life and being willing to commit to it, no matter the obstacles. It's about setting clear goals, aligning your actions with your purpose, and continually checking in with God to ensure you are on the right path. A clear vision helps you focus your energy and time on what truly matters, and it keeps you moving forward even when the journey feels long or difficult.

God has placed a unique vision in each of our hearts, and when we align our lives with His plans, we can live with purpose and meaning. Don't let distractions cloud your vision. Stay focused on the goals God has set before you, trusting that He will guide you every step of the way.

PRAYER

Father, thank You for the vision You've placed in my heart. I want to live intentionally, pursuing the path You've set before me. Help me to keep my focus on Your purpose and not be distracted by the things that pull me away from You. When the path seems unclear, give me the clarity to trust in Your guidance. Strengthen me to stay focused on the vision You've given me, knowing that You are always with me, even in the challenges. I trust that You will lead me to the right place at the right time. In Jesus' name, Amen.

INTENTIONAL REFLECTION

What is the vision God has placed on your heart? How can you take intentional steps today to align your actions with that vision?

Feel free to take a moment and write down your thoughts and ideas.

THE INTENTIONAL PURSUIT: 31 DAY DEVOTIONAL

DAY 17

WALKING IN GOD'S PURPOSE

"Many are the plans in a person's heart, but it is the Lord's purpose that prevails."

PROVERBS 19:21 (NIV)

We were all created with purpose, and living intentionally means aligning our actions with the plans God has for us. Proverbs 19:21 reminds us that while we may make many plans in our hearts, it is ultimately God's purpose that prevails. This is both comforting and challenging. It means that while our desires and ambitions are important, they must be submitted to God's greater plan for our lives.

The story of the Apostle Paul exemplifies this principle beautifully. Paul had his own plans for his life, and he was deeply committed to them. Initially, his purpose was to persecute Christians, believing he was protecting the faith. But God had a different plan for him. On the road to Damascus, Paul's life was dramatically altered when he encountered Jesus. In that moment, Paul's vision shifted from personal ambition to God's purpose. Though it was a difficult and humbling journey, Paul faithfully followed the new direction God had set for him, preaching the gospel to the Gentiles and building the early Church (Acts 9).

Just like Paul, we may have our own ideas about what we want to achieve in life, but living intentionally means trusting that God's purpose is greater than our own. It requires surrendering our plans and allowing God to guide us, even when His path looks different from what we imagined. God's purpose might not always be comfortable or easy, but it is always filled with meaning and impact. When we align ourselves with God's will, we find fulfillment and peace, knowing that we are part of a bigger story.

Living intentionally involves daily decisions to follow God's leading, even when it's unclear where He's taking us. It's about surrendering our timeline, desires, and ambitions to Him. When we trust that God's purpose will prevail, we can walk forward with faith, knowing that He is always at work in us and through us.

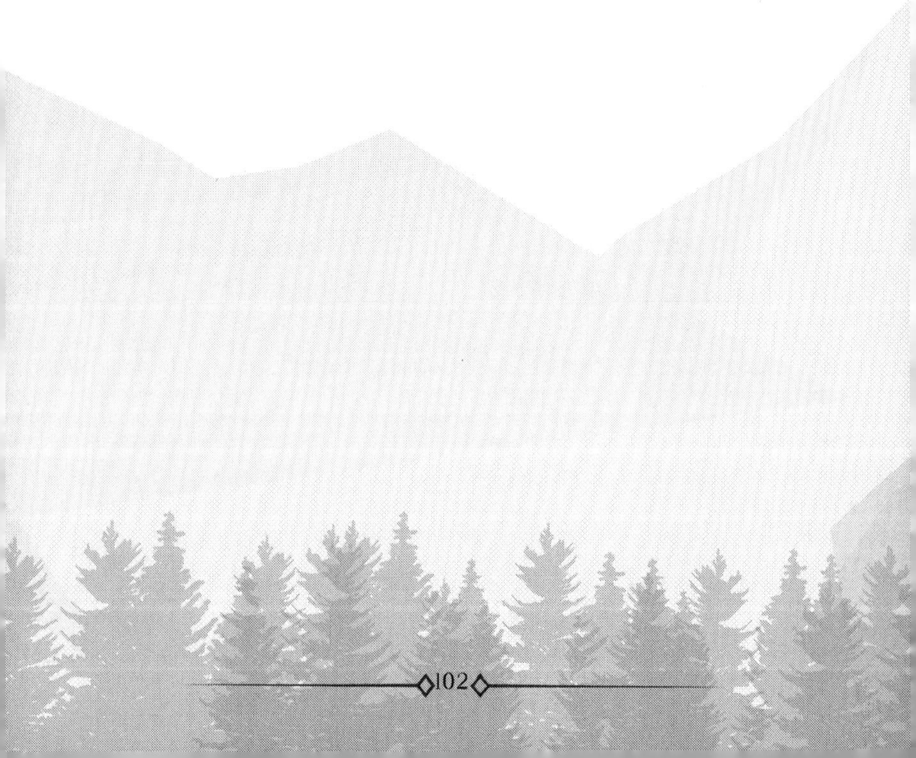

PRAYER

Lord, thank You for the purpose You have placed in my life. I confess that at times I focus more on my plans than Your purpose. Help me to surrender my desires to You and trust that Your plan is better than anything I could create. Teach me to walk in Your will, even when I don't understand the full picture. Give me the strength to follow Your lead, knowing that Your purpose for me will prevail. I choose to trust You with my journey and embrace the calling You have for me, no matter where it leads. In Jesus' name, Amen.

ERICA D. BOYD

INTENTIONAL REFLECTION

What plans in your life do you need to surrender to God's purpose? How can you intentionally align your actions with His will today?

Feel free to take a moment and write down your thoughts and ideas.

THE INTENTIONAL PURSUIT: 31 DAY DEVOTIONAL

DAY 18

EMBRACING CHANGE

"Jesus Christ is the same yesterday and today and forever."

HEBREWS 13:8 (NIV)

Change is inevitable, and often, it can feel overwhelming or unsettling. We may resist it, fearing the unknown or the discomfort it brings. However, change is also an essential part of growth. God is constantly moving us from one season to the next, and embracing these changes is key to living intentionally.

The Apostle Paul experienced dramatic change throughout his life. From being a persecutor of Christians to becoming one of the faith's most passionate advocates, his transformation was nothing short of radical (Acts 9). Paul didn't fight the changes that came with his encounter with Christ; instead, he embraced them, allowing God to shape him into a new creation. Through his willingness to adapt, he was able to serve God's purpose on a global scale.

Similarly, we are called to embrace the changes God brings into our lives. Whether it's a new job, a shift in relationships, or a move to a new place, change is often the pathway to fulfilling God's purpose. While it can feel uncertain, we must remember that God is unchanging. His faithfulness remains the same through every transition.

Living intentionally means embracing change with faith, knowing that God is using it to refine us, strengthen us, and prepare us for the next chapter. Change doesn't have to be feared; it can be viewed as an opportunity to grow deeper in faith and trust in God's sovereignty. When we lean into the changes He brings, we discover that He is always present, guiding us through each season.

PRAYER

Father, I acknowledge that change can be challenging, and it's easy to become anxious about the unknown. Yet, I trust that You are unchanging and that Your plans for me are good. Help me to embrace change with a heart of faith, knowing that You are working in every season. When change feels uncomfortable, remind me that I don't walk through it alone. Give me the strength to accept the changes You bring into my life, trusting that they are part of Your perfect plan for me. In Jesus' name, Amen.

INTENTIONAL REFLECTION

What change are you currently facing or resisting?
How can you choose to embrace it with faith,
trusting that God is using it for your growth?

Feel free to take a moment and write down your thoughts and ideas.

THE INTENTIONAL PURSUIT: 31 DAY DEVOTIONAL

DAY 19

THE IMPORTANCE OF PERSISTENCE

"Do not throw away your confidence; it will be richly rewarded."

HEBREWS 10:35 (NIV)

Persistence is a key element of intentional living. In a world where instant gratification is often expected, we may feel tempted to give up when things don't happen as quickly as we want. Yet, the Bible encourages us to persist, knowing that our efforts will bear fruit at the right time. God calls us to be steadfast, even when the journey feels long or the progress seems slow.

Consider the story of the Israelites as they wandered in the wilderness for forty years. Their journey was full of trials, and they faced obstacles at every turn. However, God did not abandon them. Despite their doubt and struggles, God remained faithful and led them to the Promised Land (Joshua 1:2-6). They had to persist through difficult seasons, trusting that God would fulfill His promises, even when it seemed impossible.

Living intentionally means staying committed to the course, even when progress feels slow or setbacks arise. Our confidence in God's promises is key. We may not always see immediate results, but the Bible reassures us that our faithfulness and persistence will eventually lead to a reward. We are called to press forward with unwavering confidence, trusting that God will complete the good work He started in us (Philippians 1:6).

Persistence doesn't mean pushing through without rest; it means continuing forward with a heart full of faith, even when challenges arise. It's about maintaining confidence in God's timing and trusting that He will see us through every season of life.

PRAYER

Father, thank You for the reminder to remain persistent. It's easy to get discouraged when things don't happen as quickly as I want. Help me to hold on to the confidence You've given me, knowing that You are faithful to fulfill Your promises. Strengthen my resolve to keep moving forward, even when the road gets tough. Teach me to trust Your timing, and remind me that You are working behind the scenes. I know that my efforts are not in vain, and I choose to keep pressing on with faith. In Jesus' name, Amen.

INTENTIONAL REFLECTION

Where in your life do you need to persevere and trust that your efforts will be rewarded? How can you hold onto your confidence in God's promises?

Feel free to take a moment and write down your thoughts and ideas.

THE INTENTIONAL PURSUIT: 31 DAY DEVOTIONAL

DAY 20

LIVING WITH PURPOSE AND CLARITY

*"The Lord will fulfill His purpose for me;
Your love, O Lord, endures forever—do not
abandon the works of Your hands."*

PSALM 138:8 (NIV)

Purpose is like a compass, guiding us through the uncertainties of life. Without purpose, it's easy to become distracted or drift through life without direction. But when we know why we're here and where we're headed, we can face any obstacle with confidence and strength.

Nehemiah's story serves as an example of a life driven by purpose. When Nehemiah heard that the walls of Jerusalem were in ruins, he was deeply moved and chose to act. Instead of simply grieving the situation, he prayed, sought God's direction, and took bold action to restore the city. Nehemiah's purpose was clear: to rebuild the walls for the protection and restoration of his people. His vision wasn't just about a physical structure—it was about the greater purpose of serving God's plan for His people.

Nehemiah encountered opposition, distractions, and even threats, yet he remained focused on his mission. His clarity of purpose kept him grounded, and in just 52 days, the walls of Jerusalem were rebuilt (Nehemiah 6:15). Nehemiah's story reminds us that living with purpose requires both clarity and persistence. It's about focusing on what truly matters, staying committed to God's will, and not allowing temporary setbacks to deter us from fulfilling the plan He has for our lives.

Living intentionally means seeking God's direction and aligning our daily actions with His purpose. It's about not allowing distractions to hinder us from pursuing what He has called us to do. Whether it's in our relationships, work, or personal lives, living with purpose requires clear focus, intentional decisions, and steadfast determination to honor God in everything.

THE INTENTIONAL PURSUIT: 31 DAY DEVOTIONAL

PRAYER

Father, thank You for the purpose You have given me. Sometimes it's easy to become overwhelmed or uncertain about the path ahead, but I trust that You have a plan for me. Just as You gave Nehemiah a clear purpose and strength to see it through, I pray that You will reveal Your plan for my life more clearly. Help me to prioritize what matters most and to remain steadfast in pursuing Your calling.

Guide my decisions and my steps, and remove any distractions that may hinder me from fulfilling Your purpose. Teach me to live intentionally each day, focusing on what aligns with Your will. I ask for the courage to keep moving forward, even when challenges arise. Thank You for being my guide and for equipping me with everything I need to live a life of purpose. In Jesus' name, Amen.

ERICA D. BOYD

INTENTIONAL REFLECTION

What is the purpose God is calling you to live out in this season of your life? How can you take intentional steps today to live more purposefully?

Feel free to take a moment and write down your thoughts and ideas.

THE INTENTIONAL PURSUIT: 31 DAY DEVOTIONAL

DAY 21

CULTIVATING GRATITUDE

"Give thanks in all circumstances; for this is God's will for you in Christ Jesus."

1 THESSALONIANS 5:18 (NIV)

Gratitude is more than a passing feeling; it's a decision we make every day. In a world that often focuses on what we lack or desire, gratitude shifts our perspective. It invites us to focus on God's goodness, faithfulness, and provision, even when things are not perfect.

The apostle Paul is a great example of someone who lived out the power of gratitude, even in difficult circumstances. Writing from prison, Paul repeatedly emphasized the importance of giving thanks, not because everything was perfect, but because God is always worthy of praise. In Philippians 4:11-13, Paul shares that he has learned to be content in every circumstance, because his strength comes from Christ. Whether in abundance or in need, Paul's heart remained thankful.

Living with gratitude means choosing to see God's hand at work in all things. It's about recognizing His blessings in the midst of challenges and trusting that even in hardship, God is present, faithful, and working all things for our good (Romans 8:28). Gratitude doesn't deny the struggles but chooses to focus on the goodness of God in the midst of them.

Living intentionally with gratitude is a choice we make daily. It's about setting aside time to reflect on God's faithfulness, to thank Him for both the big and small things, and to cultivate a heart that sees His blessings in every situation. Gratitude changes our hearts and our outlook on life. When we focus on gratitude, we shift our attention from what we don't have to what we've been given, opening the door for more joy and peace to enter our lives.

THE INTENTIONAL PURSUIT: 31 DAY DEVOTIONAL

PRAYER

Father, I come before You with a heart full of gratitude. It's easy to focus on what's missing or what's difficult, but I choose today to give thanks for Your goodness. Thank You for Your constant provision, for Your presence in my life, and for the many blessings I often overlook.

I confess that sometimes I take Your blessings for granted, and I ask for Your forgiveness. Help me to cultivate a heart of gratitude, not just when things are going well, but especially when life feels challenging. Teach me to see Your hand at work in every circumstance, and give me the strength to trust that You are always good, no matter what. I want to live intentionally with a heart of thanks, honoring You in every situation. Thank You for being faithful and for filling my life with Your love. In Jesus' name, Amen.

INTENTIONAL REFLECTION

What are three things you can thank God for today, no matter what your circumstances are? How can practicing gratitude change your outlook on life?

Feel free to take a moment and write down your thoughts and ideas.

THE INTENTIONAL PURSUIT: 31 DAY DEVOTIONAL

DAY 22

WALKING IN INTEGRITY

*"The righteous who walks in his integrity—
blessed are his children after him!"*

PROVERBS 20:7 (ESV)

Integrity is a rare and powerful quality. It's the ability to do the right thing, even when no one is watching. In a world that often rewards shortcuts and dishonesty, integrity sets us apart as people of truth, honor, and authenticity.

One Biblical example of integrity is Daniel. When exiled to Babylon, Daniel found himself in a foreign land with different customs, pressures, and temptations. Yet, he remained true to his convictions and to God. Even when faced with the choice of compromising his faith to align with the king's demands, Daniel chose to honor God rather than bow to the world's expectations. His integrity brought him favor with both God and men. In Daniel 6, despite the dangers, Daniel continued to pray and worship God, knowing that his integrity was more important than his safety.

Living intentionally means making choices that align with God's truth, even when it's uncomfortable or unpopular. It's about being consistent in our actions, regardless of the situation or who is watching. Living intentionally with integrity involves making conscious decisions every day to reflect honesty and truth in our words and actions. It's about choosing what is right when no one is looking, knowing that our integrity is a reflection of our heart and relationship with God. When we walk in integrity, we honor God and inspire others to do the same.

Integrity is not just about the big decisions, but the small, everyday choices we make. It's how we respond when no one is watching and how we treat others in private. Living intentionally with integrity means choosing what is right in every moment, no matter the cost.

THE INTENTIONAL PURSUIT: 31 DAY DEVOTIONAL

PRAYER

Father, thank You for the example of integrity found in Your Word. I want to live a life of honesty and truth, honoring You in every action and decision. Forgive me for the times I've compromised my integrity and given in to pressures that didn't align with Your will.

Help me to walk in integrity, no matter the circumstances. May my life reflect Your goodness, and may my actions honor You in everything I do. Strengthen me to make the right choices, even when it's difficult or unpopular. I want to be a person of truth and honor, both in public and in private. Thank You for being my guide in all things, and for helping me stay true to You. In Jesus' name, Amen.

INTENTIONAL REFLECTION

In what areas of your life do you feel challenged to walk in integrity? How can you make intentional choices today to align your actions with God's truth?

Feel free to take a moment and write down your thoughts and ideas.

THE INTENTIONAL PURSUIT: 31 DAY DEVOTIONAL

DAY 23

THE POWER OF CONSISTENCY

"Do not despise these small beginnings, for the Lord rejoices to see the work begin."

ZECHARIAH 4:10 (NLT)

Consistency is the quiet power behind long-term success. It's easy to start strong, but the real difference is made in how we finish. Consistent effort, even in small ways, has the ability to produce great results over time.

Consider the story of Noah. For 120 years, Noah built the ark despite ridicule, isolation, and the absence of rain. His obedience wasn't based on immediate results—it was built on his unwavering commitment to God's word. Day after day, Noah worked with purpose, and when the flood finally came, his faithfulness saved his family and countless animals (Genesis 6:9-22). His consistency in following God's command, even when it seemed nonsensical to others, paid off in the long run.

Living intentionally requires consistency in our actions. It's easy to get distracted by the noise of the world or discouraged by the lack of visible results. But the key to walking in purpose is remaining steadfast in doing good, even when we don't see the immediate rewards. Zechariah 4:10 reminds us not to despise small beginnings because God rejoices in the work we start, even if it seems insignificant at first. Our consistent actions, however small they seem, are a part of His greater plan.

Consistency doesn't mean perfection. It's about showing up every day, taking small, purposeful steps toward the life God has called us to. Whether in our relationships, work, or faith, living intentionally with consistency means making the decision each day to honor God with our time and efforts. Over time, this consistency will build a life that reflects His faithfulness and goodness.

ERICA D. BOYD

PRAYER

Lord, thank You for the example of consistency in Your Word. I know that often I become weary when I don't see immediate results, but You remind me that good things come to those who don't give up. Help me to be consistent in my faith, my work, and my relationships.

I confess that sometimes I let discouragement or impatience get the best of me. Help me to trust that my efforts are not in vain, even when I don't see immediate fruit. Strengthen me to remain steadfast and committed, knowing that You are at work in ways I can't always see. Thank You for the promise of a harvest in Your perfect timing. Help me to keep my eyes fixed on You as I continue to walk in faith. In Jesus' name, Amen.

ERICA D. BOYD

INTENTIONAL REFLECTION

In what area of your life do you need to commit to more consistency? What small steps can you take today to build that consistency into your routine?

Feel free to take a moment and write down your thoughts and ideas.

THE INTENTIONAL PURSUIT: 31 DAY DEVOTIONAL

DAY 24

TRUSTING GOD'S PROVISION

"And my God will supply every need of yours according to his riches in glory in Christ Jesus."

PHILIPPIANS 4:19 (ESV)

Trusting God's provision can be one of the most liberating aspects of living intentionally. In a world that constantly pushes us to accumulate, control, and rely on our own efforts, it can be difficult to remember that God is the ultimate provider. Yet, His provision is not just about meeting our physical needs; it extends to every area of our lives—emotional, spiritual, relational, and financial.

The story of the Israelites wandering in the desert provides a powerful picture of God's provision. Despite their complaints, doubts, and disobedience, God faithfully provided for His people. When they were hungry, He sent manna from heaven. When they needed water, He caused a rock to pour forth streams (Exodus 16-17). The Israelites didn't always understand how or why God provided the way He did, but He always met their needs, in His time and in His way.

Living intentionally means acknowledging that God's provision isn't just something He does occasionally; it's a continuous act of love. Trusting Him to provide in our lives means recognizing that everything we have comes from Him and that He will continue to supply our needs. It requires letting go of the fear of scarcity and trusting that God's resources are limitless, and that He knows exactly what we need and when we need it.

Whether we are facing financial struggles, relationship challenges, or emotional exhaustion, trusting in God's provision frees us to focus on His will and purpose for our lives rather than the anxiety of unmet needs. Living intentionally in this way means choosing faith over fear and relying on His promises, knowing that He will never leave us or forsake us.

THE INTENTIONAL PURSUIT: 31 DAY DEVOTIONAL

PRAYER

Father, thank You for Your constant provision. I confess that sometimes I get anxious about my needs and try to take control, forgetting that You are the ultimate source of everything. Help me to trust You more deeply, especially when I can't see how You will provide.

Teach me to rely on Your promises, knowing that You are faithful and that You will always provide what I need in Your perfect timing. Help me to let go of fear and control, and embrace the peace that comes with trusting You. Thank You for Your generosity and for being a God who always provides for His children. May my life reflect a deep trust in Your provision and a gratitude for all You've given. In Jesus' name, Amen.

INTENTIONAL REFLECTION

What area of your life do you struggle to trust God's provision? How can you remind yourself today that God is faithful to meet your needs?

Feel free to take a moment and write down your thoughts and ideas.

THE INTENTIONAL PURSUIT: 31 DAY DEVOTIONAL

DAY 25

THE BLESSIN OF GENEROSITY

"Give, and it will be given to you. A good measure, pressed down, shaken together and running over, will be poured into your lap. For with the measure you use, it will be measured to you."

LUKE 6:38 (NIV)

Generosity is a reflection of God's heart. It's a key aspect of living intentionally because it focuses on others, not just ourselves. When we give, whether it's our time, resources, or love, we mirror the generosity that God has shown us. We are reminded that everything we have is a gift from Him, and by giving, we participate in His work on Earth.

The widow in Mark 12 provides a powerful example of generosity. She gave two small coins, all she had to live on, and Jesus praised her for her faithfulness. Her act of giving wasn't about the size of the gift—it was about the sacrifice and the heart behind it. God sees the heart of the giver, not just the gift itself (Mark 12:41-44).

Living intentionally through generosity means making a conscious decision to bless others without expecting anything in return. It's not about how much we have to give, but about being willing to share what we do have. When we give with an open hand, we allow God to use us as conduits of His love and provision to others.

Generosity doesn't only involve material possessions—it extends to our time, energy, encouragement, and prayers. Generosity is about investing in others, knowing that God blesses those who give freely. The more we give, the more we experience God's abundant blessings, not necessarily in material wealth, but in spiritual peace and joy.

ERICA D. BOYD

THE INTENTIONAL PURSUIT: 31 DAY DEVOTIONAL

PRAYER

Father, thank You for being so generous with me. Your love and provision are more than I could ever repay, yet You call me to be generous with others. Help me to give freely, whether in time, resources, or love, with a heart that seeks to bless and serve others.

I confess that sometimes I hold back, thinking that I don't have enough to offer. But I know that when I give, You multiply the blessings in ways that I can't see. Help me to live with an open heart, eager to share what I have, knowing that in doing so, I am reflecting Your love. Thank You for the joy and peace that come from giving generously. In Jesus' name, Amen.

INTENTIONAL REFLECTION

How can you be more generous with your time, resources, or encouragement today? Who can you bless in a tangible way this week?

Feel free to take a moment and write down your thoughts and ideas.

THE INTENTIONAL PURSUIT: 31 DAY DEVOTIONAL

DAY 26

STEPPING INTO GOD'S PLAN FOR YOUR LIFE

"For I know the plans I have for you, delcares the Lord, plans for welfare and not for evil, to give you a future and a hope."

JEREMIAH 29:11 (ESV)

Every one of us is called to live intentionally, in alignment with God's divine plan for our lives. Yet, so often, we find ourselves wondering about the "why" and "how" of our journeys. We may feel lost, uncertain, or overwhelmed by the thought of stepping into the unknown. However, God's Word reminds us that His plans for us are good, full of hope, and meant to prosper us. The journey may not always be easy, but it is always purposeful.

The life of Esther offers a beautiful example of stepping into God's plan. Esther, a Jewish orphan, found herself in the palace of Persia, not by chance, but as part of God's greater plan. At a critical moment in history, when the Jewish people were facing destruction, Esther had the opportunity to use her position to influence the king and save her people. She didn't understand the full extent of her purpose at first, but she stepped into her calling with courage and faith, knowing that God had placed her in that position for such a time as this (Esther 4:14).

Living intentionally means trusting that God has uniquely equipped and positioned you for a specific purpose. Sometimes, like Esther, we don't immediately see the significance of where we are or what we're doing, but that doesn't mean we're not part of His grand plan. Just as God had a purpose for Esther's life, He has one for you. Living intentionally requires us to take steps of faith, even when we don't fully understand how the pieces fit together.

When we step into God's plan, we may not always see immediate results or rewards, but we can trust that He is guiding us every step of the way. Each decision, big or small, is part of the greater tapestry of His will. Living intentionally means surrendering our own agenda for God's, knowing that His plans are always better and far greater than anything we could imagine on our own.

THE INTENTIONAL PURSUIT: 31 DAY DEVOTIONAL

PRAYER

Lord, thank You for the beautiful reminder that You have a plan for my life, a plan filled with hope and purpose. I confess that sometimes I struggle to step into Your plan because of fear or uncertainty. I want to know exactly where I'm going, but You've called me to trust in Your guidance, even when the path isn't clear.

Help me to live intentionally, always looking to You for direction. Give me the courage to take bold steps of faith, trusting that You are leading me into a future full of hope. I surrender my plans to You, knowing that Your will is better than anything I could come up with. Teach me to embrace the journey, knowing that each step, no matter how small, is part of Your perfect plan. Thank You for being a faithful God who leads me with love and wisdom. In Jesus' name, Amen.

INTENTIONAL REFLECTION

What area of your life do you need to step into God's plan more fully? What step of faith can you take today to align yourself with His purpose for your life?

Feel free to take a moment and write down your thoughts and ideas.

THE INTENTIONAL PURSUIT: 31 DAY DEVOTIONAL

DAY 27

PURSUING JOY IN ALL THINGS

"Rejoice in the Lord always; again I will say, rejoice."
PHILIPPIANS 4:4 (ESV)

Joy is not simply a fleeting emotion; it is a deep-rooted, steadfast attitude that flows from our relationship with God. Living intentionally involves choosing joy, even when circumstances are less than ideal. In a world filled with struggles, disappointments, and heartaches, pursuing joy might seem counterintuitive. Yet, joy is a gift from God that transcends circumstances, and He calls us to find it in every moment.

The apostle Paul provides a powerful example of pursuing joy despite adversity. When he wrote the book of Philippians, he was in prison, facing uncertain outcomes and potential suffering. Yet, throughout the letter, Paul repeatedly encourages the believers to rejoice. He writes from a place of deep faith, understanding that joy comes from knowing Christ, not from external circumstances (Philippians 4:4-7). His life shows us that even in hardship, joy can be present when we focus on God's goodness and His promises.

Living intentionally means cultivating a heart of gratitude and focusing on the blessings, even in difficult times. Like Paul, we must train ourselves to rejoice, not because everything is perfect, but because God is faithful. Choosing joy is an act of the will, a decision to trust God regardless of what's happening around us. When we pursue joy intentionally, it becomes a testimony to others that true happiness doesn't depend on the world's standards but on our unshakable faith in God.

Pursuing joy is not about ignoring the struggles or pretending everything is fine. It's about acknowledging the pain, but choosing to see God's goodness in the midst of it. It's about rejoicing in His presence, His promises, and His work in our lives. Living intentionally involves choosing to find joy, not because life is easy, but because God is with us, and His joy is our strength.

THE INTENTIONAL PURSUIT: 31 DAY DEVOTIONAL

PRAYER

Father, thank You for the joy that is found in You alone. I confess that there are times when I allow the struggles of life to steal my joy. I get overwhelmed by my circumstances, and I forget that true joy comes from knowing You. Help me to live intentionally by choosing joy, even in the midst of difficulty.

Teach me to focus on Your goodness, Your promises, and the hope I have in You. Give me the strength to rejoice in all things, knowing that my joy is not dependent on my circumstances, but on my relationship with You. Help me to find joy in the small moments, the quiet blessings, and the peace You offer in every season. I choose joy today, trusting that You are with me every step of the way. In Jesus' name, Amen.

INTENTIONAL REFLECTION

What is one area of your life where you can intentionally choose joy today? How can you shift your perspective to find joy, even in the midst of challenges?

Feel free to take a moment and write down your thoughts and ideas.

THE INTENTIONAL PURSUIT: 31 DAY DEVOTIONAL

DAY 28

BREAKING FREE FROM COMPARISON

"For we dare not class ourselves or compare ourselves with those who commend themselves. But they, measuring themselves by themselves, and comparing themselves among themselves, are not wise."

2 CORINTHIANS 10:12 (NKJV)

In a world that thrives on comparison, it can be incredibly difficult to avoid measuring ourselves against others. From social media to societal expectations, we are constantly faced with opportunities to look at someone else's life and feel as if we are falling short. Whether it's comparing our achievements, looks, relationships, or even our spiritual growth, comparison can quickly lead to feelings of inadequacy, jealousy, or even discontentment. But God calls us to a different standard—a life lived intentionally, free from the trap of comparison.

The story of David and Saul offers us an insightful example of the dangers of comparison. David, a young shepherd boy, was anointed king by God, but before he stepped into that role, he faced many challenges. One of the most notable was his time in Saul's court. Saul, who was once anointed as king, became increasingly jealous of David's success. As David gained favor with the people and even defeated the giant Goliath, Saul's comparison of himself to David began to fuel his bitterness (1 Samuel 18:6-9). Saul couldn't see that David was chosen for a unique purpose, just as Saul had been chosen for his own purpose. Saul's inability to live intentionally and celebrate his own calling led him down a destructive path of jealousy and anger.

Living intentionally means embracing who God has called you to be without comparing yourself to others. When we compare ourselves to others, we lose sight of the unique purpose and gifts God has given us. The truth is, God has a specific plan for each of our lives, and His will for us is as distinct as our fingerprints. Comparison only distracts us from our own journey and hinders our ability to step into the fullness of God's calling for us.

Instead of measuring ourselves by others' successes or failures, living intentionally means focusing on God's plan for us. It means recognizing that we are fearfully and wonderfully made (Psalm 139:14) and that God has uniquely equipped us for the life He has prepared. We don't need to be someone else to fulfill God's purpose for our lives; we need to be the person He has created us to be. It's time to break free from comparison and embrace our unique calling with confidence.

THE INTENTIONAL PURSUIT: 31 DAY DEVOTIONAL

PRAYER

Father, I confess that I often struggle with comparison. I look at others and wonder why I haven't achieved what they have or why my journey doesn't look like theirs. Thank You for reminding me today that You have created me for a specific purpose and that Your plan for my life is unique and beautiful. Help me to see my value through Your eyes and not through the lens of comparison.

Teach me to celebrate the gifts You've given me, instead of wishing I had someone else's talents, opportunities, or experiences. Help me to walk in the path You've laid out for me with confidence, knowing that You are with me every step of the way. Give me the courage to embrace who I am, rather than trying to be someone else. Thank You for the reminder that I am fearfully and wonderfully made, and that You are faithful to fulfill Your plans for my life. In Jesus' name, Amen.

INTENTIONAL REFLECTION

Where in your life are you struggling with comparison? How can you shift your focus from comparing yourself to others and instead embrace the unique purpose God has for you?

Feel free to take a moment and write down your thoughts and ideas.

THE INTENTIONAL PURSUIT: 31 DAY DEVOTIONAL

DAY 29

THE POWER OF PRAYER IN ACTION

"Therefore I tell you, whatever you ask in prayer, believe that you have received it, and it will be yours."

MARK 11:24 (ESV)

Prayer is one of the most powerful tools available to us as believers, yet it can sometimes feel like an underutilized resource. Many of us know the importance of prayer, but we often view it as something passive—a time to ask God for what we need, seek His guidance, or express our gratitude. However, prayer is more than just words spoken in solitude. It's a call to action that compels us to align our hearts with God's will and take steps in faith.

The story of Nehemiah is a beautiful example of the power of prayer in action. When Nehemiah heard that the walls of Jerusalem were broken down and the city was in ruins, he was deeply moved (Nehemiah 1:3-4). He didn't just pray for the situation to change, he prayed fervently, confessing the sins of his people and asking God for favor and guidance. His prayer was not a passive request but a passionate plea for God's intervention. And, as a result, God gave him favor with the king, and Nehemiah was sent back to Jerusalem to rebuild the walls. Nehemiah's prayer led him to take action, and his faith in God's power and provision enabled him to complete the monumental task of restoring the city (Nehemiah 2:17-18).

Living intentionally in prayer means recognizing that prayer is not only about asking but also about listening, seeking God's guidance, and then stepping out in faith to do the work He has called us to do. Prayer without action can sometimes feel empty, but prayer that fuels action leads to transformation. When we pray with belief and intention, we open ourselves to God's direction, and our actions become an extension of His will on earth.

In our own lives, there may be situations where we are waiting for God to act, but He is waiting for us to take the next step. God moves in response to our prayers, but those prayers should lead to action. Whether it's starting a new project, serving someone in need, or stepping into a new season of life, our prayers should inspire us to move. We must believe that God hears us and trust that He will provide the strength, wisdom, and resources to accomplish what He has called us to do.

ERICA D. BOYD

THE INTENTIONAL PURSUIT: 31 DAY DEVOTIONAL

PRAYER

Father, thank You for the gift of prayer and the power it holds. I confess that sometimes I treat prayer as a passive act, not fully recognizing that it is meant to inspire action. Help me to view prayer as more than just words; help me to see it as a powerful force that propels me to step out in faith.

Teach me to pray with boldness and belief, trusting that You are always at work, even when I cannot see it. Just as Nehemiah's prayer led to action, I pray that You would guide me in my own life to take the steps You are calling me to. I want my prayers to be accompanied by action, for I know that it is through my obedience that Your kingdom is advanced. Strengthen my faith and give me the courage to move when You lead. In Jesus' name, Amen.

INTENTIONAL REFLECTION

What is one area of your life where you feel God is calling you to pray and then take action? How can you step out in faith and trust that God will provide the strength and wisdom you need?

Feel free to take a moment and write down your thoughts and ideas.

THE INTENTIONAL PURSUIT: 31 DAY DEVOTIONAL

DAY 30

LIVING OUT YOUR CALLING

"For we are His workmanship, created in Christ Jesus for good works, which God prepared beforehand, that we should walk in them."

EPHESIANS 2:10 (ESV)

Living out our calling can be one of the most fulfilling aspects of our lives, yet it can also feel daunting and overwhelming. Often, we look at others who seem to be walking confidently in their calling, and we wonder if we are missing the mark. But the truth is, each of us has been uniquely designed and called by God to fulfill a purpose that is greater than ourselves. The challenge is not in discovering that calling, but in being faithful to walk in it, even when it feels unclear or difficult.

The story of Esther is a profound example of living out one's calling. Esther, a Jewish orphan, was placed in a position of power as queen of Persia. At first, it may have seemed like a fortunate turn of events, but Esther's position was not just for her benefit—it was for the saving of her people. When the Jewish people faced the threat of annihilation, Esther had to step into her calling and take action, despite the personal risks involved. Her uncle Mordecai reminded her of her unique position: "Who knows whether you have not come to the kingdom for such a time as this?" (Esther 4:14). Esther's response was a powerful example of intentional living—she fasted, prayed, and took bold steps to stand up for her people, trusting that God had placed her in that position for a reason.

Esther's story teaches us that living intentionally involves recognizing that our current circumstances, relationships, and opportunities are not by chance. God places us where He needs us, and He equips us for the tasks ahead. Living out your calling doesn't always mean dramatic moments or public recognition—it often means showing up faithfully in the ordinary moments of life and being obedient to what God asks of us.

Living intentionally means taking the time to listen for God's voice and following His lead, even when it's uncomfortable. It means embracing the calling He has placed on your life, whether big or small, and trusting that He will equip you for the journey. You don't have to wait for a "perfect moment" or a grand sign to step into your calling. God has already equipped you with everything you need—now, it's time to act with purpose.

ERICA D. BOYD

THE INTENTIONAL PURSUIT: 31 DAY DEVOTIONAL

PRAYER

Father, thank You for the unique calling You have placed on my life. I confess that sometimes I feel uncertain about my purpose or doubt that I am equipped for the task at hand. Yet, I know that You have created me for good works, prepared in advance for me to walk in. Help me to see my life through Your eyes and recognize the opportunities You have placed before me.

I pray for the courage to step into my calling with confidence, even when the path is unclear or difficult. Just as You gave Esther the strength to stand in the face of adversity, I ask that You give me the boldness to live intentionally for Your glory. Help me to trust that Your timing is perfect, and that every moment is part of Your divine plan. Teach me to walk in obedience to the calling You have placed on my life. In Jesus' name, Amen.

INTENTIONAL REFLECTION

What is one area of your life where you feel called to step out in faith and live intentionally? How can you begin to act on that calling today?

Feel free to take a moment and write down your thoughts and ideas.

THE INTENTIONAL PURSUIT: 31 DAY DEVOTIONAL

DAY 31

THE INTENTIONAL PURSUIT

"I press on toward the goal to win the prize for which God has called me heavenward in Christ Jesus."

PHILIPPIANS 3:14 (NIV)

As we arrive at the final day of this devotional, we reflect on what it truly means to live with intentionality. Living with purpose is not a fleeting aspiration or a one-time decision. It's a lifelong commitment, a daily pursuit of the goals God has set before us. Each moment, each choice we make, carries with it an opportunity to align ourselves more closely with God's will and to fulfill the purpose He has placed on our lives.

The apostle Paul's words in Philippians 3:14 challenge us to press on toward the goal. But what does this goal look like? It's not just about achieving success or accomplishing tasks. It's about walking in the fullness of God's plan for us, becoming who He created us to be, and bringing glory to His name through our lives. It's a call to live with conviction, to run the race of life with perseverance, and to embrace every opportunity to grow deeper in our relationship with Christ.

Paul's life provides us with an inspiring example of intentional living. Despite facing countless hardships—imprisonment, rejection, shipwrecks, and beatings—he remained steadfast in his pursuit of

God's calling. He didn't allow circumstances to define his purpose. Instead, he pressed on, focusing not on the temporary struggles, but on the eternal prize awaiting him. He understood that his calling was far greater than his present challenges and that the ultimate reward was not in earthly accolades, but in knowing Christ and fulfilling the mission God had entrusted to him.

Living intentionally means embracing this same perspective. It means looking beyond the immediate circumstances and fixing our eyes on the eternal. The challenges, the setbacks, and the detours are all part of the process. But they do not define us—they refine us. The pursuit of God's call requires perseverance and resilience. It demands that we keep moving forward, even when the road seems uncertain, because we know that each step is leading us closer to the prize: a deeper relationship with God, a life that reflects His love, and a purpose that brings His kingdom to earth.

Living intentionally is about living with vision and purpose. It's about asking ourselves every day: "What is God calling me to do today? How can I serve Him today? How can I grow in my relationship with Him today?" It's about making conscious decisions to pursue God's will in every area of our lives—our work, our relationships, our health, our finances, and our spiritual walk. Intentionality is not passive. It is active. It is choosing to align our actions, thoughts, and priorities with God's purpose for us.

And while the pursuit is important, it's not about perfection. We are not expected to have it all figured out. The beauty of the intentional pursuit is in the journey itself—the constant growing, learning, and trusting. There will be times when we stumble, when we question, when we doubt. But the key is to keep pressing on, to keep our focus on the ultimate goal, knowing that God is faithful to complete the work He has begun in us (Philippians 1:6).

When we live intentionally, we invite God into every moment. We allow Him to shape our decisions, guide our steps, and transform our hearts. This pursuit is not about striving in our own strength, but about surrendering to God's leading. It's about trusting that He will equip us for every task, strengthen us for every challenge, and bless us in every step of the journey.

As we come to the end of this devotional, let this final day serve as a reminder that the pursuit is far from over. The intentional pursuit of God's purpose is a lifelong journey. And every day we are given a new opportunity to press on, to deepen our relationship with Him, and to make a lasting impact in the world around us. Our lives can be filled with purpose and meaning, not because of what we achieve, but because of the God we serve and the life we live in response to His call.

THE INTENTIONAL PURSUIT: 31 DAY DEVOTIONAL

PRAYER

Father, thank You for bringing me to the end of this devotional and for reminding me that intentional living is not just a season, but a lifelong pursuit. As I reflect on the journey I've taken these past 31 days, I recognize that the path ahead still requires effort, focus, and trust. I acknowledge that it is not always easy to press on when life gets hard, when challenges arise, or when the road feels uncertain. But I choose to trust in You, knowing that You are with me every step of the way.

Help me to press on toward the goal, just as Paul did, even when the path is difficult. Strengthen my heart and my faith as I pursue the calling You have placed on my life. When distractions arise, help me to refocus on You and the mission You've entrusted to me. When doubts creep in, remind me of Your promises and the eternal prize that awaits me. When I feel weary, carry me and give me the strength to keep moving forward.

Lord, I surrender my plans, my desires, and my timeline to You. I want to live intentionally, to walk in Your will every day, and to serve You with my whole heart. Help me to seek You first in everything I do and to trust that You will lead me where I need to go. Thank You for Your unfailing love, Your constant guidance, and Your perfect plan for my life. I press on, with purpose and confidence, knowing that with You, nothing is impossible.

In Jesus' name, Amen.

INTENTIONAL REFLECTION

What is one specific action step you can take today to ensure that you are living intentionally in pursuit of God's plan for your life? How can you continue to press on in this pursuit beyond this devotional?

Feel free to take a moment and write down your thoughts and ideas.

THE INTENTIONAL PURSUIT: 31 DAY DEVOTIONAL

This final day is not just the end of a devotional, but a reminder to keep pressing forward in the intentional pursuit of God's purpose for your life. Keep your eyes on the goal, and never stop moving forward with faith, hope, and perseverance.

BONUS DAY: DAY 32

RELEASING CONTROL TO GOD

"Trust in the Lord with all your heart, and lean not on your own understanding; in all your ways submit to him, and he will make your paths straight."

PROVERBS 3:5-6 (NIV)

One of the most challenging aspects of living intentionally is learning to release control to God. In a world that emphasizes self-reliance and personal control, it can feel uncomfortable to surrender our plans and trust that God's way is best. We often believe that if we don't take control, things will fall apart, or we'll miss our opportunities. But living intentionally doesn't mean clinging tightly to our own agendas—it means acknowledging that God is sovereign over all things and trusting Him with our lives.

The story of Abraham and Isaac is a profound illustration of releasing control to God. God called Abraham to do something unimaginable—sacrifice his only son, Isaac, the child of promise. In Genesis 22:2, God tells Abraham, "Take your son, your only son, whom you love—Isaac—and go to the region of Moriah. Sacrifice him there as a burnt offering on a mountain I will show you." This was not only a test of Abraham's obedience but also a test of his trust in

God's character. Abraham had to release control of the situation and trust that God's plan was better than his own, even when it didn't make sense.

Abraham's willingness to follow God's command, even in the face of unimaginable pain, shows the depth of his faith and surrender. In the end, God provided a ram as a substitute for Isaac, showing that He had a better plan all along (Genesis 22:13-14). Abraham's obedience in releasing control to God resulted in a profound display of God's faithfulness and provision.

Living intentionally means letting go of our need to control every aspect of our lives and trusting that God knows what is best. It means submitting our desires, our fears, and our future to Him, knowing that He holds all things in His hands. When we release control, we make room for God to work in ways we can't even imagine. It's not about giving up on our dreams, but about entrusting them to God's timing and wisdom.

When you release control, you are saying, "God, I trust You with my life. I trust that You are good, and that You are working everything together for my good and Your glory." Let go of the need to micromanage and surrender your plans to the One who holds the future.

THE INTENTIONAL PURSUIT: 31 DAY DEVOTIONAL

PRAYER

Father, I confess that I often struggle with releasing control to You. I want to have everything figured out, but I know that I cannot do it on my own. Thank You for reminding me that You are in control, and that Your plans for me are good. Help me to trust You more deeply with my life, my plans, and my future.

Teach me to surrender my fears and desires to You, and to submit to Your will in all things. Just as Abraham trusted You with the life of his son, help me to trust You with every area of my life. Show me where I am holding on too tightly, and help me to release control, knowing that You will make my paths straight. I choose to rest in Your wisdom and Your perfect timing. In Jesus' name, Amen.

INTENTIONAL REFLECTION

What area of your life have you been holding onto control in? How can you begin to release it to God and trust His plan for you?

Feel free to take a moment and write down your thoughts and ideas.

THE INTENTIONAL PURSUIT: 31 DAY DEVOTIONAL

AFFIRMATIONS OF INTENTIONALITY

I am intentional in my thoughts, actions, and decisions, aligning them with God's will for my life.

Every step I take is purposeful, moving me closer to God's calling and plan for me.

I choose to live with clarity, focusing on what matters most and letting go of distractions.

I trust in God's timing, knowing that He is guiding me even in the waiting seasons.

I am committed to living a life of purpose, embracing the journey with faith and confidence.

My actions reflect my values, and I honor God in all I do.

I embrace each day as an opportunity to grow, learn, and live intentionally.

I am bold and courageous in pursuing God's plan
for my life, no matter the challenges.

I choose gratitude in every circumstance, seeing
God's hand at work in all things.

I trust that God's purpose for me is greater than
any fear or uncertainty I may face.

I release perfectionism and choose progress, trusting
that God will lead me to what I need.

I align my goals and desires with God's will,
knowing He equips me for every good work.

I am filled with peace as I live intentionally, knowing
that each day is a step toward fulfillment.

I choose joy and contentment, even in the process
of pursuing God's plan for my life.

I am surrounded by God's love, and it fuels
my journey toward intentional living.

I let go of comparison and trust that my path
is uniquely designed by God for me.

I believe in the power of prayer and use it to guide
my decisions and strengthen my purpose.

I am resilient, and through God's strength, I overcome
any obstacles in my pursuit of His will.

I walk in obedience, knowing that God is faithful
to fulfill His promises in my life.

I am an active participant in God's plan, and I take intentional
steps each day to move closer to my purpose.

AFFIRMATION PRAYER

Lord, I thank You for the strength, clarity, and wisdom to live intentionally each day. I affirm that I am walking in Your purpose, trusting Your timing, and choosing to align my actions with Your will. May these affirmations serve as reminders of my commitment to living for You, and may they guide me as I continue on this journey of intentional pursuit.

In Jesus' name, Amen.

CLOSING THOUGHTS

As you've walked through these 31 days of reflection, prayer, and intentional action, I hope you've experienced a deepening of your faith and a renewed sense of purpose. Living intentionally means more than just checking things off a to-do list. It's about aligning your heart, mind, and actions with God's will, and embracing the journey with faith, patience, and perseverance.

Remember, intentional living doesn't end after these 31 days—it's a lifelong pursuit. Each day is an opportunity to grow, to step forward with confidence, and to walk in the abundant life that God has called you to. Keep your eyes on His purpose, remain open to His leading, and never stop seeking the joy that comes from living fully aligned with His plan.

God has great things ahead for you, and as you continue in the pursuit of His will, know that He walks with you every step of the way. You are not alone in this journey, and He is always with you, guiding you, strengthening you, and leading you into the fullness of His promises.

CLOSING BLESSING

May you be filled with the peace that surpasses all understanding, the courage to pursue God's calling with clarity and focus, and the strength to live each day with purpose and intention. May you trust in God's perfect timing, rest in His promises, and boldly step into the life He has planned for you.

As you continue your journey of intentional living, may you be a light to others, reflecting His love and grace in all that you do. May your steps be guided by His wisdom, your heart led by His truth, and your actions fueled by His power.

Go forth in confidence, knowing that the God who has begun a good work in you will carry it to completion.

In Jesus' name, Amen.

Made in the USA
Columbia, SC
03 February 2025

52490040R00115